My Many Hats

My Many Hats

Juggling the diverse demands
of a music teacher

Richard Weymuth

HERITAGE MUSIC PRESS

A DIVISION OF THE LORENZ CORPORATION
Box 802 / Dayton, OH 45401-0802
www.lorenz.com

Editor: Kris Kropff
Type Design: Digital Dynamite, Inc.
Cover Design: Jeff Richards

Heritage Music Press
A division of The Lorenz Corporation
P.O. Box 802
Dayton, OH 45401-0802
www.lorenz.com

Printed in the United States of America

ISBN: 0-89328-197-2

Contents

Acknowledgements

Dr. Annelle Weymuth, my wonderful wife and patient proof-reader.

D.J. and Jeanette Weymuth, our outstanding son and daughter-in-law and my computer gurus who less-patiently proof-read this book.

Olivia Weymuth, "The Most Beautiful Granddaughter in the World," for always loving PaPa.

Bill and Virginia Bateman, Bateman Photography, for the excellent photography.

Mary Lynn Lightfoot, a great music editor and tremendous friend.

Kris Kropff, the greatest book editor I know.

Introduction

This book started as a project in a doctoral class at the University of Miami, Coral Gables, Florida, in the fall of 1977, when I was given the assignment to develop a research project on some facet of teaching excellence. I chose to look at master teachers and how they achieved their successes.

During one interview with a master teacher, while discussing tasks, concepts and goals, it came to me to ask if they felt that they wore different hats at different times in the classroom. This led to a research project called, *Hats of a Teacher*.

Since that time, I have developed a presentation where I wear fifteen different hats, each integral to the teaching profession. I have given this presentation over a hundred times at many local, regional and national conventions. Through these presentations I have worked with thousands of students, as well as new and seasoned teachers. I have had an opportunity to hone my presentation over time, and continue to feel validated that my hats are on target even as curriculums and educational philosophies change. There are specific traits of a master teacher that never change. There are specific hats that are essential for the young teachers to learn.

It is a true art to see a master teacher at work; one that has fascinated me throughout my life and provided me with the model that I wanted most to emulate. Analyzing the amazing skills of these true heroes of the classroom—those that motivate and mold students—is not an easy task.

The fifteen hats presented in this book are my best attempt to emphasize the greatest skills of these master teachers. Each of these teachers wears many hats in a class period, in a school year, in a teaching career. I have discovered that the greatest teachers know what hat to wear, what time to wear it, and when the hat should be removed. Most teachers are wearing several hats at any given time. Mastering this balancing act is the dream of every teacher who strives for excellence.

My philosophy is that anyone who goes into teaching must love working with students. They need to be motivated to go to the classroom each morning simply because they love seeing the "light bulb go on" in the students' eyes or face as they comprehend and learn a new concept or understand a new idea. I love to watch students grow and achieve. I can only hope that my presence in the classroom has been a small part of their love for learning.

I want my hats to put a smile on your face as you read this book, just as they do for the airport security guards as they go through my bags at the airport. They ask, "Are you a magician? A clown? An entertainer?" My answer is, "Yes, I am a teacher."

The Hat of a

Ringmaster

1

The Hat of a

Ringmaster

The hat of the ringmaster is the first and most important hat of them all. As an educator striving for excellence, you must often don the top hat of the ringmaster while at the same time continuing to manage your own three-ring circus. Once this hat is mastered, you will be able to easily handle the diverse abilities and activities found in the typical music classroom.

As a teacher, you may be thinking, "In ring one, we have a group of students who are working on advanced music concepts with a new music software program. In ring two, we have Mary and James, who were recently ill and need to take their make-up exams. In ring three, a small group of students needs additional help with sight reading." To top it off, in the back of your mind you hear, "Now ladies and gentlemen, we have waiting to enter the tent the remainder of our class as they return from their research project in the library. They will be moving into ring…"

Great teachers are organized. They make sure that each ring is full and active. Well-organized teachers have effectively mastered lesson plans, to-do lists and time management, and they avoid procrastination at all costs. By mastering these four skills, organization will naturally follow and the result will be a reduction or elimination of discipline problems, as well as an ability to keep all the activities in your room going strong.

Lesson Plans

Outstanding teachers have a well-prepared, written lesson plan. Master teachers often spend an extensive amount of time preparing and writing detailed, innovative lessons. By having the lesson well prepared, the teacher is able to mentally run through it, add or delete content, and practice the delivery, thus eliminating potential problems. By doing so, you not only ensure the success of that one lesson, you now have a well-developed lesson to use year after year.

A teacher that doesn't properly prepare and "shoots from the hip" tends to face a lack of respect and interest from the students, and will often have discipline problems in the classroom. In addition, the students quickly notice whether the teacher is prepared and will tend to model his or her behavior. So, practice what you preach. If you want your students to do their homework, then you need to do your homework before the lesson.

To-do List

A comprehensive to-do list helps keep the teacher on task. Unlike the written lesson plan, this is an abbreviated list of what is to be covered or accomplished today. This essential list can serve as a road map to ensure that all major points and concepts are covered.

You will find this list to be extremely helpful if a discipline problem should arise and your focus temporarily changes. The list allows you to get right back on track. By keeping your daily lists, you will also be able to easily review what was covered in class to assist a student who was absent.

Time Management

Efficient use of classroom time is an absolute necessity because dead time in the classroom creates opportunities for discipline problems. It is imperative that you use every moment of class time for instruction, review, practice, work, etc. If you as the teacher do not value every moment of class time, your students will not value it either. The safest way to keep students focused and on track is to prevent them from getting off track.

How can you punish a student for being late to class if you don't start class on time? The best answer to this obviously rhetorical question is that you, the teacher, should be on time and require the students to always be on time. The teacher that permits students to be a minute late the first week of school will find that the one minute will increase to two, then three, then ten. The best teachers plan and use every moment of the time allocated each day.

Avoid Procrastination

The master teacher does not procrastinate. Whether it is teaching specific concepts, returning a call to a parent, or thoughtfully disciplining a student, the teacher must complete the task in a timely manner.

Procrastination may also occur on a larger scale. For example, many new teachers only think a few weeks ahead, as opposed to a few months ahead, when preparing for an upcoming performance. Compounding this problem is the tendency to lose track of rehearsal time or underestimate the time it takes to prepare for a concert performance. Adding procrastination to this already tenuous balance can have a disastrous result.

Take ordering music. The process of ordering music is a "do-it-now" task. You must order the music so that it arrives at least eight weeks before the concert. Occasionally, music will be temporarily out of stock or permanently out of print (POP). You must be so organized that you have a back-up plan in case your do-it-now task can't happen when you need it to happen, but you also must give yourself enough time to implement that back-up plan by tending to the do-it-now tasks now.

Students cannot and do not succeed when the teacher is unorganized or has not given them adequate time and materials for success. A great teacher wears the ringmaster hat to keep students busy and on task. Organization is the key to success, and it is accomplished with good planning, comprehensive lists, efficient use of time, and by avoiding procrastination.

I touch the future, I teach.

—**Christa McAuliffe**

If you fail to plan, you are planning to fail.

—**Robert Schuller**

8 My Many Hats

The Hat of a

2

I'M THEIR LEADER

WHICH WAY DID THEY GO?

Leader

2

The Hat of a
Leader

The classroom leader sets the direction and tone of the classroom. More than just outlining your vision for the class and working toward it, the direction and tone are most often set by the choices you make when presented with multiple directions in which to lead the class. This dilemma is reflected in the Robert Frost poem "The Road Not Taken": *Two roads diverged in a yellow wood, and sorry I could not travel both…*

Leading for the Long Term
It is up to you to select the proper road for your classroom. Teachers will travel down the road and often come to a major fork. It is up to the leader to decide which road they will all travel, and consequently to accept the joys and consequences

found along that road. Unfortunately, the easiest road for the teacher to travel down is too often the "popular" or "fun" road.

Traveling on this road allows the teacher to gain quick popularity and sometimes allows him or her to more easily lead the class. The great educator, however, will select, "the other road, the one less traveled." The road less traveled often takes longer and requires more work, but ultimately reaps the biggest rewards.

While on the road less traveled, you will not always be the most popular or fun teacher, but you will earn the respect of your students. It is often said that students will live up to your expectations. Set your expectations low and your students will always reach them, but set your expectations high and—through hard work, perseverance and dedication—your students will earn a strong educational foundation and respect you.

Bumps in the Road

You, as the teacher, know the correct path to success, and it is up to you to guide your students to and along that path. You are inventive enough to creatively avoid the various diversions and detours that you will encounter and you are able to move the class to *your* ultimate destination, yet it is essential to keep the class on task and to encounter a minimum number of diversions and roadblocks.

You *will* receive numerous suggestions for improving your program from your fellow teachers, students and friends. Many times the suggestions will be ideas you do not wish to use, but on occasion you will receive a suggestion that will improve your program. As a good teacher, be willing to take the good ideas and modify them to fit your program accordingly.

You *will* have days you plan to accomplish many objectives, but due to weather, holiday breaks and other unforeseen reasons, class does not go as planned. Remember, sometimes you have to go with the flow. The world won't end if you don't get your Bach lesson presented that day.

The outstanding teacher will proudly wear the hat of a leader and will relate to the closing words of Robert Frost's "The Road Not Taken": *I took the one less traveled by, and that has made all the difference.*

I suppose that leadership at one time meant muscle; but today it means getting along with people.

—Indira Gandhi

Excellence is never an accident.

—H. Jackson Brown, Jr.

The Hat of a

3

Scholar

B

The Hat of a

Scholar

The hat of a scholar is worn by every master teacher. The difficulty when wearing this hat is determining how much time it must be worn during each class period. Excessive wear can create boredom and cause problems, yet the hat of a scholar must be worn often enough for academic substance.

If only a minimal amount of time is devoted to scholarship, the students will not receive adequate information, thus their test scores will not be as high as you would desire. Also, the students will lack the necessary background to execute a given concept to its highest potential. On the other hand, if you wear the hat of a scholar for an excessive amount of time, the students may become bored and "turned off." Furthermore, too much detail can obscure the important elements of the concept or lesson.

Finding the Right Balance

Innately, the master teacher seems to know exactly how much time the scholar hat needs to be worn. He or she seems to be able to present enough scholarly information to ensure proper academic challenges, yet not so much as to turn the students off to the concepts that must be presented. The master teacher seems to have a sixth sense for knowing how much time is appropriate.

Unfortunately, new teachers, fresh from university music classes, often want to teach too much academic material. For example, an entire class period dedicated to "The Important Aspects of the Time and Life of Wolfgang Amadeus Mozart" is too much for even high school students. For the lesson to be great it must include important aspects of the life of Mozart yet still capture the attention of the students. Avoid replicating lessons you enjoyed in college. Instead, make the information unique to your specific class.

Scholarship in the Information Age

In today's world, the hat of the scholar is often challenged by the students, but it needs to be worn during all class periods. In a world where the student is accustomed to the fast-paced, short bursts of information such as television and the Internet, the teacher has to make sure that scholarly information is presented creatively. Innovative presentations are a necessity when presenting difficult, essential concepts, especially in subjects that the students refer to as "dull and boring."

Master teachers know the magic amount of time to wear the scholar's hat to ensure success. With hard work, dedication and a bit of creativity, you, as a new teacher, will soon learn when and for how long to wear your scholar's hat.

Every day is lost in which we do not learn something useful. Man has no nobler or more valuable possession than time.

—Ludwig van Beethoven

A teacher should know more than he teaches, and if he knows more than he teaches, he will teach more than he knows.

—Anonymous

The Hat of a

Disciplinarian

4

The Hat of a

Disciplinarian

The hat of a disciplinarian is an essential hat for any teacher but is especially important for a new teacher. And unfortunately, an eight-foot bullwhip is not a tool you can use in the classroom.

When perspective teachers were asked what gives them the greatest concern or worry as they plan for their first teaching position, 2,480 out of 3,000, or over 80%, answered discipline.[1] Even though young teachers overwhelmingly state this concern, most universities and colleges don't give enough practical experience in the art of effective discipline.

---

[1] Henry Clay Lindgren, *Educational Psychology in the Classroom* (New York: Wiley & Sons, 1971) 372.

Not So Real World

Universities often require observation classes and student teaching to provide their students with a real-world teaching experience, but they usually place their students with master teachers; master teachers who, by virtue of their excellence, have the fewest discipline problems. Over a ten-year period, I observed student teachers and found that this was overwhelmingly true. The students who were placed with master teachers didn't have to deal with the same discipline problems as those with other, less-experienced teachers. When I asked the student teachers why this gap existed, their typical response was that the students respected the master teacher, thus they did not challenge their student teacher.

Working with a master teacher helps prospective teachers greatly, but it also puts them in a very controlled environment that ensures temporary success without requiring the hard work that many teaching positions will require. It is unfortunate that the current system does not place them in actual discipline situations that a first-year teacher will typically experience. Many new teachers have a rude awakening in their first teaching position when they have to deal with real discipline issues.

Establishing Classroom Rules

The first step in become a successful disciplinarian is to put in place an effective set of classroom rules. Some guidelines to consider:

- Rules must be pertinent to the age of the student receiving them.
- The teacher must be able to enforce any rule that he or she writes.
- All rules must be in accordance with and complement any school or district rules.
- All classroom rules should be written in the positive rather than the negative.
- Rules should be stated clearly and specifically so the students easily understand them. They must be written in "black and white" terminology because students do not function in shades of gray.
- Rules must be logical; students do not need "stupid rules."
- A careful balance in the number of rules is very important. Too many rules get in the way of an education; too few rules may not cover the needed facets of discipline.

It should also be noted that many master teachers feel their students better follow the rules when they had some say in them. As a teacher, you can move the rules in the direction you choose and ultimately have the rules you desire while still giving the students a sense of ownership and participation.

A Little Help From Your Friends

Because every teaching situation is unique, it is important to have in place a process for dealing with specific discipline problems rather than trying to list countless rules to cover every situation. My advice to new teachers is to develop professional relationships with second- and third-year teachers. These educators probably have more recently handled a similar situation and can be consulted for advice and assistance.

The following questions and statements were developed to help first-year teachers define problems and create these helpful contacts.

- What is the specific discipline problem that is currently bothering you?
- Who could you interview in your educational community to help with this problem?
- What is the background of the person helping you?
- How many times did this discipline problem happen to them during their first year of teaching?
- How did they handle the problem?
- What discipline solutions worked and what didn't work?
- Have you thanked the person for their time? Make sure to thank them with a gift of candy, dinner or a gift certificate. Then, take time to write a note letting them know how their recommendations helped you during your first year. (Remember, you may need to ask for help in the future.)

The Three Cs

Within the application of classroom rules, the best advice for the new teacher is to remember The Three Cs: Caring, Consistency and Control.

Caring

Caring about one's students is imperative. The impact of that caring on a personal level should never be minimized. The student who likes the teacher, and believes the teacher likes them, will learn more effectively and create fewer discipline problems than the student who does not like the teacher. New teachers must not sacrifice their goals in an effort to encourage students to like them more. Many teachers want their students to like or love them, but it is best to strive for caring and respect.

Consistency

Consistency—in application of discipline, temperament and expectations—is the second "C" vital to creating classroom discipline. Any specific rule a teacher makes must be adhered to and, if broken, addressed with consistent punishment. Unfortunately, some new teachers forget this. For example, in a choir classroom with a new teacher, a detention was given to a student for breaking a rule. A few weeks later, an outstanding male singer broke the same rule, but the teacher was not consistent in the punishment. This time, she laughed and said, "Joe, I know you didn't mean to do that, please don't do it again." In one quick moment, the student who served the detention lost all respect for that teacher. When teachers are not consistent, the door to major discipline problems is opened and students may become disillusioned, frustrated and resentful.

Be prepared for some frustrating days and try to avoid losing your temper. A consistent temperament will help the year go more smoothly for you and your students. Also, be consistent with your expectations for the students. If you ask a student to do something, make sure you follow through. A young teacher was working with her students when one of the young male singers refused to sing. Frustrated, she quickly said, "If you don't sing, the entire class will sit here until you do." Like the typical high school boy, he refused to sing and the end of class was quickly approaching. Not wanting to lose face in front of the other students, she quickly came up with a win-win solution. She asked some of the football players in the choir if they would mind singing with the boy so the rest of the class could leave. The football players agreed; the boy sang along. Fortunately, with some quick thinking, the teacher turned a potentially nasty situation into a positive one, with the outcome she desired. Consistency is essential for new teachers.

Control

The third "C" is control. No new teacher can do a good job teaching, nor can the class learn, unless the teacher is in control of the class. One of the qualities that all good teachers possess is the ability to maintain an exciting yet orderly class. Ineffective teachers are unable to control their class.

The Three Cs—Caring, Consistency and Control—are absolutely essential to successful discipline. To have a wonderful year of minimal stress and few discipline problems, let the students know that you are caring, consistent and in control.

The teacher must always be on the attack looking for new ideas, changing worn-out tactics, and never, ever falling into patterns that lead to student *ennui* [boredom].

**—Pat Conroy,
The Water Is Wide**

Talent without discipline is like an octopus on roller skates. There's plenty of movement, but you never know if it's going to be forward, backwards, or sideways.

—H. Jackson Brown, Jr.

The Hat of an

Eagle

5

The Hat of an

Eagle

The eagle hat represents the "eagle eye" that every successful teacher must have, use and hone, for it will prevent many problems before they start. There are two main reasons to master the eagle eye. First is the stare that master teachers possess. This look can make the student stop, melt and cease any challenge to the teacher's power. Second is the ability to predict behavior infractions and problems before they start.

Stare Down

A master teacher has an unbelievable ability to totally control a class with the eagle eye. For many new teachers the eagle eye is natural, while some new teachers must practice until it becomes natural. It is important to note that the effectiveness of the eagle eye will be neutralized by laughter or non-serious body language. An example: a first-year teacher entered the room to find that one of his students had climbed into the classroom rafters. The teacher quickly tried to take control of the situation by using the eagle eye, only to start laughing a few seconds later. Even worse than not resolving the immediate problem, this teacher lost the power of "the eye" for the rest of the year. Once you lose the eagle eye, it is almost impossible to get it back with those students.

Seeing Into the Future

As a teacher, you must constantly listen and analyze your students' behavior and evaluate other factors such as grade level, socioeconomic level and classroom diversity in an effort to predict what they'll do next. For those of you that had mischievous tendencies as a student, you may already be a step ahead and can predict what you might have done as a student in the same situation. If you are lucky enough to have this talent, then there shouldn't be a thing your students can get away with. If you were one of the class angels, then this is a skill you will need to develop.

Listening carefully, coupled with some on-the-mark predictions, can convince students you have eagle eyes in the back of your head, too. By just listening and reacting, you can cut down on many problems and, depending on the grade level you teach, scare the others into behaving. A good example of a first-year teacher's successful employment of this technique was when she said, "Excuse me tenors, I assume we are paying attention?" while her back was to the class. When the teacher later turned around and looked pointedly at the two boys who had been talking, both were fully re-focused on the lesson. In one quick moment, she handled the problem in a very positive way.

As a new teacher, you control your own destiny when wearing the hat of an eagle. Use it carefully and consistently. Don't play favorites, using it with some of the students and not with others. The students will quickly identify the students that are treated differently. The eagle eye can't solve all of your first-year teacher problems, but it can help make you more successful in the classroom.

A teacher is one of the most special people in the world, for who else could spend day after day giving of themselves to someone else's children?

—Deanna Beisser

It is not fair to ask of others what you are not willing to do yourself.

—Eleanor Roosevelt

The Hat of a

Crab

6

The Hat of a

Crab

The hat of a crab should be worn only rarely, serving to remind the teacher that being crabby and negative in the classroom will create a group of students who are crabby and negative. It is important to remember that your attitude and behaviors are mirrored by your students. You set the mood of the classroom and are responsible for keeping the mood positive.

It has often been said that positivism ignites positivism and negativism ignites negativism. During my 30-plus years in education I found this to be very true. I have had the opportunity to observe numerous high school teachers and what I found was that a negative statement to a choir, like "Tenors, will you quit singing flat!," did little to correct the choral problem whereas one positive statement, like, "Way to go tenors, keep working hard, lift those eyes, and now think the pitch higher," quickly elicited the desired effect. By turning the negative statement into a positive, the students felt successful and challenged rather than hurt and rejected.

Being positive is one of the greatest ways to build a strong program and improve the self-esteem of the choir. Goethe wrote, "If we treat people as they are, we make them worse. If we treat people as they ought to be, we help them become what they are capable of becoming." New teachers with their exciting, positive approaches can turn a choral program around, thus creating a positive classroom where a negative situation had formerly existed.

How to Treat a Student

The following eight points will assist in building a positive choral program as well as the students' self-esteem.

- Call each student by his or her name.
- Listen to the students attentively.
- Take an appropriate level of personal interest in the students.
- Plan lessons to ensure success.
- Focus on what the student has done correctly, rather than on his or her mistakes.
- Use constructive criticism with all students.
- Be patient and tolerant with all students.
- Respect the feelings of all students. Never embarrass a student in front of his or her peers.

And from Dr. Hiam Ginott's *Teacher and Child*:

- I have come to the frightening conclusion that I am the decisive element in the classroom.
- It is my personal approach that creates the climate.
- It is my daily mood that makes the weather.
- As a teacher, I possess tremendous power to make a [student's] life miserable or joyous.
- I can be a tool of torture or an instrument of inspiration.
- In all situations, it is my response that decides whether a crisis will be escalated or de-escalated and a child (student) humanized or dehumanized.[1]

The hat of a crab should remind each new teacher that the world is often crabby and it is our job to *avoid* wearing this hat as much as possible. Although occasionally, the hat of crab must be worn to emphasize displeasure so the class comes to the understanding that the current situation will not be condoned. Students and teachers both need to relate to the mantra—*positivism ignites positivism and negativism ignites negativism.*

---

[1] Hiam G. Ginott, *Teacher and Child: A Book for Parents and Teachers* (New York: Macmillan, 1972) 15–16.

Your mind can only hold one thought at a time — make it a positive and constructive one.

—H. Jackson Brown, Jr.

The bad teacher's words fall on his pupils like harsh rain, the good teacher's, as gently as the dew.

—Talmud: *Ta'anith, 7a*

The Hat of a

Juggler

7

The Hat of a
Juggler

The hat of a juggler is a well-worn hat for all music teachers, for they must constantly balance numerous activities both in and out of the classroom. It takes a master juggler to keep each day an organized and exciting educational experience.

No teacher is busier or a better juggler than a K-12 vocal music teacher. (Don't say you'll never do this because one never knows where or what he or she many be teaching in five or ten years.) An actual schedule of a K-12 vocal music teacher who taught in three different buildings, located in three different small towns, appears on the following page.

		Monday	Tuesday	Wednesday	Thursday	Friday
High School	7:45 a.m.–8:35	General Music or Choir				
	8:35–9:00	Travel				
	9:00–9:30	5th – A	4th – A	5th – A	4th – A	K – A
Elementary School	9:30–10	5th – B	4th – B	5th – B	4th – B	K – B
	10–10:30	3rd – A	2nd – A	3rd – A	2nd – A	1st – A
	10:30–11	3rd – B	2nd – B	3rd – B	2nd – B	1st – B
	11–11:30	K – A	K – B	1st – A	1st – B	Planning*
	11:30–11:50	Lunch				
	11:50–12:05 p.m.	Travel				
	12:05–12:15	Setup				
Middle School	12:15–1:05	7th – A	7th – B	7th – A	7th – B	Rotate A & B
	1:10–2	6th – A	6th – B	6th – A	6th – B	Rotate A & B
	2:05–2:55	8th Grade General Music or Choir				
	2:55–3:10	Bus Duty				
Depart	3:30					

*Some states require 60 minutes of planning time per day. Although the only dedicated planning time in this schedule is 30 minutes on Fridays at the Elementary School, this school district uses the two travel/lunch blocks, which total 60 minutes, to meet the requirement.

The teacher may leave the building at 3:30, but we all know this doesn't happen often!

A schedule like the above begs the questions:

- When does the teacher have time to put away the high school equipment? Will other teachers have use of the room during the day?
- When does the teacher take out the Orff instruments at the elementary school?
- When does the teacher remove the Orff instrument bars and get other materials ready for class?
- With five consecutive elementary classes, when does the teacher get supplies ready? When does the teacher take a restroom break?
- Does this schedule really meet the state requirement for preparation time?

These are just a few of the many concerns of a new teacher. One new teacher told me that his position also required the maintenance of three different bulletin boards. At one of the schools, the principal required a new, seasonally appropriate bulletin board on the first day of each month.

The Grass Is Always Greener

While at first glance it may seem that a high school teacher who teaches in one building only has a simpler schedule, this is not the case at all. As a high school vocal music teacher, you have a different preparation every hour. You are always trying to balance sight reading with quick rote learning. You are balancing rehearsals for numerous school concerts, assemblies and school "run out" concerts (performing at local venues).

The teachers must also think about obtaining buses for "run outs" and trips, selecting new choral literature, and purchasing new show choir outfits. Then it is time to start rehearsing for the all-school musical, knowing it shouldn't take class time since every student in your class is not in the musical. You may also have your annual, semi-annual or quarterly fund-raising activities.

To help make financial ends meet, some teachers accept a church or temple choir position, and then start to worry about how this extra work will balance with school activities. As if this is not difficult enough to balance, some of the students will request private voice or piano lessons outside of class time.

Once you are able to handle all of this, you will have earned the hat of the juggler. Even though juggling isn't easy, a career as a vocal music teacher is one of the most rewarding in the world. You touch the lives of so many students who learn to love music because of the amazing juggling you do.

The harder you work, the luckier you get.

—Gary Player

The difference between a job and a career is the difference between forty and sixty hours a week.

—Robert Frost

The Hat of a

Banker

8

The Hat of a
Banker

The hat of a banker is vital for the survival of any music teacher. In a poll asking why new music teachers did not have their contracts renewed, one of the top three reasons was the inability of the teacher to manage money for fund-raising activities and budgets. Many teachers become so involved in teaching, discipline and motivation that they forget the precision needed for monitoring fund-raising activities and budgeting requests for their programs.

Fund Raising

Fund raising within the music department can be a salvation for the program or a disaster that destroys it. In an ideal world, school boards would give every music teacher sufficient money to create and sustain an excellent program. Unfortunately, we are not living in an ideal world and you, as the banker, must fund raise in order to have adequate materials and money to create an excellent program.

Unfortunately, many schools have to look to fund raising just to preserve their choral programs. Depending on the school, you will find some that only have to do one fund-raising activity a year, while others fund raise each semester, quarter or more. The golden rule of fund-raising activities is: *receive maximum profit utilizing minimum time.*

The following guidelines should be considered when fund raising:

1. Carefully review a list of possible fund raisers to find the activity that will best fulfill the golden rule.
2. The teacher's time should be used to instruct during class time, not to become a bank cashier.
3. Use choir officers to collect money and pass out additional products. Always make sure that there are at least two officers working at a time. This minimizes the possibility of lost money and protects the students.
4. There should be a one-page record for every student, kept in a loose-leaf notebook, to be filled out by the officers when they take the money or check out product. For efficiency, have a separate binder for each class or choir. This must be checked by the teacher after each school day. By checking this daily, you are sending the students a message that they are accountable for accuracy in their records.

5. The teacher must motivate the students, excite them, and create in them a desire to participate in the fundraising activity. Appropriate prizes or gifts can be added as an extrinsic motivation. These prizes or gifts could be given to the student that makes the most sales, makes the biggest profit, etc. Group rewards, such as a pizza party, could be given to all students who meet their sales goals, or to the class that performs the best in relation to their goals.

6. A detailed final report should be formulated showing profits, student sales, and a brief summary of the "success" of the sale. For example, mention the students that won awards and classes that performed extremely well. Finally, briefly describe how much you enjoyed the project and how you appreciate the administration allowing you to do this. Distribute this to the appropriate administrators.

7. If possible, plan your fund raiser at the optimal time of the year. Grapefruit and orange sales are perfect during the winter months. A candy sale over Thanksgiving break is ideal because visiting relatives buy from the students. Think about the target audience for your fund raiser as you plan your sales to make the most of your time and effort.

It would be beneficial if teachers possessed business degrees, but we don't, so do your best and remember that there are many master teachers you can turn to for help you if you need it.

Planning and Administering a Fund-raising Activity

The following tips and questions to ask yourself will be helpful when organizing your fundraiser:

- Secure permission for the activity from the administration.
- What is your goal for the fund raiser? What fund raiser offers the greatest opportunity of achieving that goal?
- On what date(s) should the activity occur/begin and why?
- Detail the steps that must be taken prior to the activity.
- Detail the kick-off drive.
- Post and distribute information about the fund raiser: important dates, procedures, prizes, etc.
- How is activity administered? Product distributed? Money collected?
- Should stock remain following the activity? How do you handle excess product? Can it be returned?
- Detail the culminating event for the activity (party, prize giveaway, etc.).
- What prizes and incentives are to be offered? What are my available resources for prizes?
- Detail the final accounting of the activity.
- Present the final accounting and report it to the administration.

Possible Fund Raisers

Interviews with choral directors from successful choral programs revealed the following list of successful fund-raising activities.

Sales

Brooms
Candy
Candles
Christmas ornaments/
   wrapping paper/bows
Cleaning supplies
Cookie dough
Eggs
First-aid kits
Flowers
Fruit
Fruit cakes
Light bulbs
Magazines
Mulch
Pizza
Popcorn
School supplies
T-shirts

Events

Bake Sale
Carnival
Car Bash
Car Wash
Community Garage and
   Rummage Sale
Computer Dating
Dinner Theatre
Ice Cream Social

Other ideas

Hand-delivered paper hearts
   and/or flowers with
   personalized messages
Raffles
Recordings of your concerts
   (remember to secure all
   appropriate licenses)
A school- or community-
   themed cookbook
Singing telegrams

Motivating Students to Sell, Sell, Sell

As mentioned above, extrinsic motivations will encourage your students to get involved in the fund raiser. The examples below are based on a candy sale, but the concepts translate well to most fund raisers.

Set goals

Establish a goal for each class, i.e. sell 16,000 boxes of candy. Host a pizza party for the class that sells the largest percentage of its goal.

Create tiered individual goals. For example:

1. Sell at least 15 boxes the first weekend of the sale and receive a poster.
2. Sell another 6 boxes (21 total), receive a mug or poster.
3. Sell another 4 boxes (25 total), receive another mug or poster.
4. For every 25 additional boxes you sell, you'll receive another mug or poster.

Raffle a daily prize, like a stuffed animal. Each student receives 1 ticket/entry blank for every 10 boxes sold.

Offer major prizes for the top-ten salespersons. The first-place salesperson selects his or her prize first, then the second-place seller, and so on. Some ideas for major prizes include:

- Watch (Men's)
- Watch (Women's)
- iPod
- CD player

- Small television
- Basket of popcorn treats
- $50.00 gift certificate to J.C. Penney
- $50.00 gift certificate to a gas station
- $100.00 gift certificate to a local movie theater
- $75.00 gift certificate to Wal-mart

Prizes

Go into the community and work with the boosters to secure both the smaller prizes, like posters and mugs, which can be created with a custom design each year, and the more significant prizes. These may seem extravagant, but you never know what you'll get until you ask. If you receive cash donations, go shopping. You may want to ask a few student officers for ideas about the best prizes.

Tracking

Provide each student with a sheet to track his or her sales. Blanks should be provided for the student's name, phone number and class schedule, as should a grid with the following columns:

- Date
- Boxes check out
- Boxes paid for
- Boxes still in possession
- Prizes issued
- Running total of boxes sold

Budgeting

Another important responsibility when wearing the banker's hat is that of budget planner and financial administrator. There are many types of budgets used within school districts, but the one you must worry about is the zero-based budget. This is by far the hardest budget for a new teacher to comprehend. In a nutshell, a zero-based budget means you start with zero and build from there, receiving only what you justify in your detailed budget request. (Obviously, it would be hard for a new teacher to know what he or she will need the first year, as is required for zero-based budgeting, but by the end of the first year the teacher will be able to plan easily for the next year.)

It is important that you justify, in detail, every item in your budget request, regardless of budget type. Remember, all teachers in the school are competing for the same pot of money. Your requests must be more detailed than the requests of other faculty members in order to receive the greatest amount of your requested budget. And always read the fine print. Some administrators require the teacher to request needed amounts of paper, pencils, chalk, erasers, and all other classroom supplies. This is in addition to the cost of music, sound equipment, uniforms, and travel needs.

Budgeting and fund raising are difficult and require reviewing previous expenditures, looking at past fund raisers, as well as figuring out costs for future programs. With a bit of hard work and creative planning, your program will be everything you dream of it. Budget for today; plan for tomorrow!

Friendship is like a bank account: you cannot continue to draw on it without making deposits.

—Anonymous

If you think education is expensive, try ignorance.

—Derek Bok

The Hat of an

9

Artistic Director

9

The Hat of an

Artistic Director

The hat of an artistic director expands and fully demonstrates the creative side of every good music teacher. Universities teach creative elements in music, but unfortunately, almost no university teaches you how to be creative with non-musical elements such as choir outfits, costumes, brochures, publications, etc.

For example, a new male vocal music teacher—top in his graduating class—takes his first job. He's excited, rosy cheeked and unstoppable, with an "I can do anything" attitude. The first week of school, the PTA president approached him to ask about his design for the show choir dresses, because her daughter wanted to be in show choir. He was floored and didn't know what to say; his university had never taught him anything about show choirs, let alone how to design their outfits.

This young music teacher quickly learned that he had to expand his creativity beyond his musical training. In addition to designing the show choir dress and vests, he was responsible for all concert program covers. He also had to expand his creativity to creating bulletin boards for each of his three classrooms.

Show and Concert Choir Dress

Show and concert choir outfits can cause major problems, as this new teacher quickly learned when he tried to make selecting outfits a democratic decision. He thought that a committee of students to plan the outfits was a good idea. A verbal war ensued between two different cliques that were represented on the committee. Each group wanted an outfit that looked the best on their friends, not necessarily what would look good on all of the girls in the choir. Therefore, the teacher ended up paying a professional seamstress to arbitrate the selection to ensure that the dress looked good on most of the girls.

Tips and Suggestions

- The teacher must be in charge of the choir outfit design and purchase.
- Asking for assistance from a professional is always a smart decision.
- When ordering your outfits, use a company that offers varied sizes and matching articles in both men's and

boy's sizes. The company must also offer matching outfits for women in junior, petite, misses, and plus sizes.

- If you are making or having your outfits made, get a
written contract stating the delivery date and that all
of the material will be the exact same color.

- If purchasing an outfit from a design company or man-
ufacturer, require a written contract that the exact outfit and color will be available for the number of years
you plan to use this outfit.

- Have someone who has skills in fitting clothing mea-
sure each student. Do not trust students to be accurate
when asked to give their clothing sizes.

The Musical

The year progressed well for this young teacher until the winter
vacation, when he sat down with the principal to discuss the
spring musical. This event was specifically listed in his contract
as his responsibility. When he asked the principal who would
design and build the sets, who would procure the props and
furniture, and who would design and install the lighting? The
principal smiled and said, "You're the man."

No university class had taught this new teacher about selecting and producing the musicals. The challenge is to select an
appropriate musical for your specific school situation. It is obviously helpful to have seen numerous shows and/or to have
sung in some of them. It is also helpful to consult resources,
like the books listed in Appendix A, along with mentors and
colleagues.

How to Select a School Musical

When selecting a musical, there are a number of factors to consider. These include:

1. What are the voicings of the solo characters?
2. Do we have students in the school that can adequately fulfill all parts?
3. Is the setting feasible for our facilities?
   a. Stage
   b. Orchestra pit
   c. Wings
   d. Fly space
   e. Lighting
4. Can we build the sets, and will they fit in our performance area?
5. Can the scenery changes be facilitated in our performance area?
   a. Behind the curtain
   b. In front of the curtain
   c. In the wings
6. Are the properties attainable and feasible in our community?
7. Can we fulfill the lighting requirements and the special effects that are needed?
8. Is the costuming feasible in our community?
9. Is the subject matter and language appropriate for the school and community?
10. Is the stage manger's guide available from the company? (This valuable book will help you address specific needs of a particular show.)

Typical Costs

You must also consider if the musical is economically feasible. Expenses can vary greatly from show to show, but will typically include:

- Royalty fees
- Rental or purchase of orchestra parts and conductor's score
- Rental or purchase of librettos, chorus parts and director's score
- Costumes
- Lighting
- Props and properties
- Scenery
- Advertising
- Printing of tickets and programs

It is the supreme art of the teacher to awaken joy in creative expression and knowledge.
—Albert Einstein

It is easy to consider the essential role of creativity in bringing joy and meaning to the human condition—without creativity we have no art, no literature, no science, no innovation, no problem solving, and no progress.

—Alane Jordan Starko

The Hat of a

Lobster

10

The Hat of a
Lobster

The hat of a lobster, though comical in looks, is a very serious hat. The lobster hat depicts that if your claws pinch the wrong places, you will be boiled in hot water. In times when teachers are accused of sexual harassment, it is very important that your hands are not perceived as being in inappropriate places. The new teacher must learn what is and is not permissible when interacting with students.

The Challenge
Sometimes a new teacher is only four years older than the seniors and may feel closer to the students than to his or her fellow teachers. Many young teachers wear the same style of clothing as the students, listen to the same music, and enjoy the same activities. The students often feel closeness to this

young, stylish, new teacher, and desire to know him or her better outside of the classroom.

The new teacher should use good judgment in communicating with students outside of school. If a private meeting must occur outside of school, decide on a restaurant or other very public place. At no time should the new teacher—especially if single—permit the students to come to his or her home, or go anywhere alone with a student. Even if you are extremely close with the family of this particular student and feel that you know them very well, always involve a group when doing things with students, be it inside or outside of school.

What Can Happen

Two new young female teachers that grew up in big cities found their first teaching positions in a small rural community. Even though it had been recommended to the young teachers to live in a nearby city so they could have a more active and private social life, they chose to live together in the small town where they taught. As the months progressed, they found their only friends were their hard-working, talented senior students.

One Friday evening after a basketball game, the two young teachers invited some of the seniors over to their apartment. The female students felt they should not go so the only students attending were the males. One of the boys took some alcohol and by Monday morning the entire town knew about the "the party." Both teachers were placed on leave and were later released from their contracts. They also lost their teaching licenses and can never again teach in that state. This was a very harsh reality for two young teachers who forgot to wear their lobster hats.

Do the Right Thing

As a teacher, you should strive to always be respected by your students. Being liked by them is great, but respect should be the ultimate goal of all teachers, new and master alike. Remember that your students also want you to like and respect them. Showing them that you care about them without violating important and necessary boundaries can be a very difficult task.

For a teacher in the elementary school, make sure you ask your students if they want or need a hug before giving them one. As the students get older, a handshake and verbal compliments are appropriate. You must be aware that some students and/or parents may take an innocent touch the wrong way and make a major incident out of it.

It is important to always wear the hat of a lobster when you are around students, thus reminding yourself that if your claws pinch the wrong place, you will be in boiling water.

The world belongs to the enthusiast who keeps cool.

—Williams McFee

When I was a boy of fourteen, my father was so ignorant. I could hardly stand to have the old man around. But when I got to be twenty-one, I was astonished at how much he had learned in seven years.

—Mark Twain

The Hat of a

Pirate

11

The Hat of a
Pirate

Just like a pirate, you are searching for your treasure, or at least a job you will treasure. This hat is one that will be extremely important to wear when you start your first job search. You must sell yourself to the principal and others who interview you so they will offer you a contract for their school.

The pirate hat should also be worn if you plan to change jobs. As a teacher in your first position, though, you should attempt to stay in a district for a minimum of three years. This shows future employers that you are a stable teacher and are dedicated to the district. Because of this, the pirate hat should not be worn often, but since change is sometimes good, don't be afraid to wear it when you need to. That goes for getting out of a difficult situation you may have found yourself in that shows little or no chance of improving, too.

The Application Process

Applying for a teaching position has many phases. First is the written part of the application process, which includes the cover letter, the résumé, and ultimately, the thank-you letter. These application skills are taught by universities, but included in this chapter are a few tips that may help you rise above the other candidates.

When a director of personnel was asked how she selects candidates from the hundreds of résumés that she received annually, her answer was as follows: "They must jump out at me. They must be perfect! Absolutely no spelling or grammatical errors are tolerated. Quality watermark paper is a necessity both for the cover letter and the résumé. While reading the materials, it must be apparent that the candidate is highly qualified, loves children, and wants more than anything else to teach."

This administrator really hit a lot of important factors. It is your job to present yourself as the best person for the position, and one who happens to also have excellent writing skills. Remember, the quality of your writing and the neatness of the presentation is what will open the first door to the interview. I was once told about a student who used bright orange paper to catch the administrator's eye. This is not a particularly good idea, although I must admit that the candidate did get an interview out of it.

Cover Letter

A cover letter with a résumé is a must. When the administrator opens the envelope, the cover letter is usually the first thing to be seen and read. It serves as an introduction to you. The cover letter must be a personal document that is brief, articulate and interesting, and contains many action words that describe your qualities as a teacher. This is your chance to hook the administrator and make him or her *want* to read your résumé.

Résumé

The résumé is usually on one sheet, but may be longer for music teachers who typically have extensive background experiences that need to be detailed on a résumé. Your résumé must be perfect because, like it or not, it may only get a thirty-second quick scan before being sorted into one of three piles: "yes," "no" or "maybe."

Many school districts are moving towards or have fully embraced online applications. While this has been a blessing for many personnel departments, it has made it more difficult to get your résumé and application materials noticed. Instead of going to a desk, as a typical résumé would, it is now stored on the school district's servers, waiting for principals to access it.

The question in the electronic age is, "How do you get your résumé noticed by the principals?" First, it is important to choose a basic font that is standard on most computers. These include Times New Roman, Verdana and Arial. While more creative fonts may add "pop" to a printed résumé, they can easily lead to disaster in a online résumé if those fonts aren't available on the principal's computer. Errant spacing, different margins and page breaks are but three of the formatting problems that can be created by a forced font substitution. The ultimate result— the principal will be looking at a jumbled collection of words.

When working on your résumé for online applications, it is important to remember that principals often search the database using keywords. So, as you are writing your online résumé, put yourself in the role of administrator and think about the qualities, characteristics and skills you would look for in an exceptional music teacher. Make sure to include those descriptive words in your résumé.

Your résumé (online or traditional) must include (in order of importance):
- Name
- Current and permanent addresses
- Phone number where you can always be reached
- Objective as an educator
- Educational background (university attended)
- Honors and awards
- Previous experiences (especially for those with a music background)
- Outstanding achievements from college or university
- References (Many applicants list specific references, with contact information, while others state, "Available upon request." If references were required as a separate attachment in the application packet, be sure to state that on the résumé.)

The Interview

After you have made it over the first hurdle and have been called for an interview, you must get prepared. You must make this first interviewer know that you are "God's Greatest Gift as an Educator," and that he or she *must* hire you.

Make a Good First Impression

Some administrators say that they make the decision about a second interview during the first 60 seconds of an interview. The candidate then has 29 minutes in which to lose the second interview with inadequate answers. Utilize appropriate body language to show you are confident and can do this job better than anyone else.

It is also important to have a professional appearance. Consider the following suggestions, and always remember to do a final, 360-degree check in a full-length mirror before you walk out the door.

- Hands and nails must be clean and well manicured. Consider unscented hand lotion if your hands are rough or dry. Ladies, keep nails professional; avoid garish polish.
- Ladies, makeup should be conservative yet attractive, and never overdone. Gentlemen, a clean shave is a must; many administrators associate personal neatness with classroom neatness.
- Hair should be neat and understated.

- Avoid perfume or cologne, as fragrance allergies are common. Do remember deodorant, though, as perspiration is a common physiological response to stress.
- Clothing should be professional but not formal; you shouldn't look like you're going out for a night on the town. Conservative, business styling in traditional colors is the way to go.
- Your clothing must fit properly. If necessary, visit a tailor.
- Shoes should be polished and complement your outfit. (One superintendent stated that he would never hire a male teacher who didn't polish his shoes.)
- Jewelry should be conservative. Gentlemen should consider removing any earrings.

The First-Class Interview

These 20 important points will help ensure a first-class interview performance.

1. Go to the interview unaccompanied.
2. Allow yourself plenty of time to get to the interview. Plan to arrive at least ten minutes early.
3. Check your appearance in the mirror.
4. Be positive, never impatient or nervous.
5. Greet the administrator with a smile and facial excitement.
6. Use confident body language.
7. Address the administrator by title and last name.
8. Shake the administrator's hand firmly.
9. Have a positive attitude, or you can forget the job.
10. Be seated only after you are told to do so.

11. Put your briefcase or purse on the floor, never on the administrator's desk.
12. Never have gum, candy or tobacco products in your mouth.
13. Be polite and never interrupt.
14. Have your portfolio of accomplishments on hand in case they are requested by the administrator.
15. Always tell the truth; lies can be prosecuted.
16. Be sincere and enthusiastic.
17. Be articulate.
18. Answer each question completely.
19. Thank the administrator and leave on time.
20. Send a thank-you letter. Other people are vying for this job. If your thank-you letter arrives first, it will be a positive indication of prompt follow-through and professionalism.

Frequently Asked Questions

The administrators will usually have a standard list of questions that they ask during the thirty-minute interview. Many of these are general educational questions although some specific questions on the major teaching area may be included.

Many of the questions typically posed by administrators during a first interview are listed on the next two pages.[1]

---

[1] Jack Warner and Clyde Bryan with Diane Warner, *Inside Secrets of Finding a Teaching Job* (Indianapolis: Park Avenue Publications, 1997) page 116–124. This wonderful book continues with 71 other frequently asked questions. It also includes the sections, "What they're really asking" and "Tips." It is a must for your library!

1. What is your greatest strength as a teacher?
2. What is your greatest weakness?
3. What can you tell us about yourself?
4. What is your philosophy of classroom discipline?
5. What steps would you take with a student who is disruptive in the classroom?
6. What kind of classroom-management plan do you like best? How would you implement it in your classroom?
7. Why do you want to be a teacher?
8. Why do you want to teach in this district/school?
9. Why should we hire you for this position?
10. What are your goals in education? Where do you see yourself five years from now? How does this position fit into your career plans?
11. What would we see if we walked into your classroom?
12. What are some trends, issues and methodologies in education that relate to your specific curriculum area or grade level?
13. What book are you currently reading or have you read recently?
14. What are some of your hobbies or leisure-time activities?
15. What special skills or talents will you bring to your classroom?
16. Would you be willing to teach at a different grade level (elementary) or teach a different subject (secondary)?
17. Would you be willing to pursue an extra certificate or credential?
18. What is your philosophy of team teaching?

19. What were you hoping we would ask today, but didn't?
20. Do you have any questions for us?

The Second Interview

When preparing for a second interview, return to "The Interview," re-read and repeat, as all of these guidelines and suggestions are equally applicable for a second interview. It is also important to compile a list of questions that you would like to have answered before you would accept this position. These questions should help you discover if this position offers you a proper fit with the right administrator, the right schedule, and the right environment. If your questions are not answered in the course of the interview, ask the administrator if he or she would mind taking questions from a list you have compiled.

The following are only a few of the important questions that you may have as a new teacher. They are offered to stimulate your thinking and encourage further questions of your own.

- Do I have a specific music room, and may I see it?
- What kinds of cross-cultural activities do you offer in your school?
- Am I responsible for a musical?
- Does the school have a mentoring program for new teachers?
- Does my evaluation and retention depend solely on my music contest ratings?
- Are parents involved in school activities?

- Is there a specific district curriculum in the music department?
- How do you describe current student morale in the music department?
- Is the music department permitted to have fund-raising activities if extra money is needed? Is the music department well funded?
- Does the school district require professional growth hours?

I would also suggest that it is a good idea to prepare this list of questions for the first interview, even though you may not have the opportunity ask them. If you create this list for the first interview, be sure to revisit and, if necessary, revise, prior to your second interview.

The hat of a pirate represents the first major hurdle of your career. Once you have that first position, it's time for you to show the teaching world what amazing things you are capable of doing.

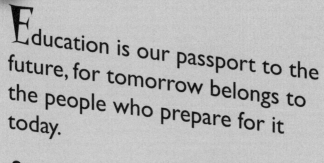

Education is our passport to the future, for tomorrow belongs to the people who prepare for it today.

—**Malcolm X**

I think that part of what you need to do to be a good teacher is to be able to imagine the lives of your students and to respond compassionately to that, and through that compassionate response, make a decision that they are worthwhile and that they are bringing something to the experience, and that you as the teacher have an important role in shaping them.

—**David Haynes**

The Hat of a

Bear

12

The Hat of a

Bear

The bear hat represents "grin and bear it," which is what new teachers must do when working with that unbearable teacher, principal or administrator. While I hope it is the least-worn of our fifteen hats, I also hope that you really know when and how to wear this extremely important hat.

Jealousy

As a new teacher, you work very hard to establish a wonderful program that truly is student centered, academic and fun. When you achieve a major breakthrough in the classroom, the students will occasionally show you appreciation by giving you warm thanks or a token gift. When this happens, you find yourself in a state of euphoria largely because you probably never expected your students to appreciate the hard work you do, let alone give you a gift. Your excitement leads you to the teacher's lounge the following morning to show your new gift to the teachers there. Unfortunately, and quite inadvertently, your action likely created resentment among some teachers or administrators because of the popularity it displayed.

This actually happened to a first-year teacher who was given a new watch by her choir as thanks for all the hard work that went into preparing for her first Winter Concert. The next morning she ran into the teacher's lounge and proudly showed her new watch to her colleagues. There were a few teachers in the lounge that thought the students' gift was wonderful and praised and congratulated her for an exceptional first Winter Concert. Sadly, there were a few teachers who had never received accolades from a class and became very upset that the new teacher received a watch. One of the veteran teachers in the building didn't speak to her for two and a half years. With this kind of jealous teacher, you have to "grin and bear it." No matter how much the new teacher tried, the older teacher held a grudge and refused to communicate with her. Of course, it would have been smarter for the new teacher to just wear the watch, but we all know how exciting it is to receive a heartfelt gift.

No, no; Thank you

In addition to difficult colleagues, occasionally you have an administrator who has run the building the same way for many years and absolutely does not want new ideas, especially from a new teacher. If you find yourself in this situation, you must "walk softly and carry a big music stand." It always pays to help the principal think that your awesome program is due in part to his or her leadership. It's smart to let the principal take credit for your new ideas. Remember, the principal is the one that writes your evaluation, and you are not yet a tenured teacher. In most states, the principal does not have to give a reason for your termination and does not have to tell you why you are not returning unless you are a tenured teacher. Let the principal shine, knowing that the parents and students know who the true hero is.

If you have a principal that takes credit for your hard work, just smile. Do not allow this type of administrator to drive you out of education. If the principal is overly demanding, caustic or difficult, it is time to apply for a transfer within the district. If a transfer is unavailable and you are miserable, move to another school district. Remember, the vast majority of principals are supportive, excellent and proud of your hard work and dedication.

When "Bearing It" Just Won't Cut It

In one school district, a very insecure administrator—who was on record saying, "No new teacher ever receives a perfect evaluation from me"—hid a tape recorder in the closet of a young teacher in an attempt to catch her making a mistake that could be used as a violation in the teacher's formal evaluation. This behavior is over the line, if not illegal. If you find yourself in a similar situation, it may be a time to stand up for yourself and seek out the support and help of a higher-level administrator. Remember that when you "go over the head" of a principal you must have an excellent reason. You will need thorough documentation and be ready to face any possible consequence. As a new teacher, you must carefully select your battles and decide what you can live with and what you want to fight to change.

It is my hope that you'll never need to wear the "grin and bear it" hat during your career. Should you run into negative teachers or principals, remember to wear the hat proudly. Keep a smile on your face, knowing you are the true caring teacher and will be a winner in the classroom.

The proud man counts his newspaper clippings—the humble man his blessings.

—Bishop Fulton J. Sheen

Education is the ability to listen to almost anything without losing your temper or your self-confidence.

—Robert Frost

The Hat of a

13

Peacock

13

The Hat of a

Peacock

If you truly want to be a teacher, then you teach because you love working with young people. You have a desire to help students be successful in your subject matter. The hat of a peacock represents you, the teacher who is "proud as a peacock" of your students.

The new teacher that can say, "I have the best students in the world," "I look forward to going to school each day," and/or "I am so glad I decided to become a teacher," will have a better year than a teacher who always puts down his or her students, school and/or teaching situation. In addition, the students who like their teacher and believe that the teacher likes them will learn more and create fewer discipline problems than those who do not like their teacher.

Get Involved

Many teachers who are "proud as a peacock" of their students have the desire to become active in additional school and community activities. Elementary teachers often conduct enrichment sessions at the end of the school day. The biggest problem with these sessions is that they often conflict with the students' transportation arrangements. Some of the students who want to take advantage of this extra help have no way to get home. The teacher has to be willing to stay until the parents can pick up the students. The teacher could take the students home but, because of the extremely litigious society we live in today, it is discouraged. Also, many districts have rules against teachers transporting students. If you wish to conduct additional after-school activities, they must be planned and approved before they are offered.

The caring middle school or high school teacher that wants to be active in the school life may volunteer to keep score at ball games, help with play rehearsals, announce at events, or become involved in other ways. This teacher may also choose to become a sponsor of the student council or other student clubs. The involvement in school and/or community activities will show your students that you are as "proud as a peacock" of them. This involvement in activities will also serve another purpose: the recruitment of new students. Other students in the school will notice your caring ways and want to be included in the excitement of your music program.

Team teaching is another way of showing pride in your students. Some great ways to integrate music into the general curriculum are to speak to the music history of a specific period, work with the foreign language teachers to help the students learn songs in different languages, or help the physical education teachers with the music for dance classes. While these activities do take extra time in your already busy schedule, they show pride in your students and help recruit new singers.

No Good Deed Goes Unpunished

Unfortunately, this pride and extra effort may make others jealous. One new elementary vocal music teacher truly became a pied piper in his school. The students worshiped his every move, always listening and never creating discipline problems. In this school there were many latchkey children who did not want to go home to an empty house. Since the students loved the music teacher so much, they congregated in the music room after school for one more fun musical activity and then helped the music teacher put away equipment before going home.

The principal of this pied-piper teacher was so jealous that he created a new school rule that stated that all children must immediately leave the school building at the end of the school day. The new teacher felt even worse about this situation when those same students started leaving the building as directed by the principal only to wait in the cold by teacher's car to say goodbye. This new teacher wisely decided it was best to leave the school at the assigned time, only to return a half an hour later, after all the students had left, to finish his work.

A master teacher, whether young or old, loves teaching students, and more than anything else, this type of teacher is truly as "proud as a peacock" of his or her students.

You can't give people pride, but you can provide the kind of understanding that makes people look to their inner strengths and find their own sense of pride.

—Sister C. Waddles

Nothing was ever achieved without enthusiasm.

—Anonymous

14

The Hat of

Applause

14

The Hat of

Applause

You have worked hard for four or more years in college, and now it's time to go out in the real world and be a winner. You are ready and eager for your first job. Like this hat, believe in yourself and applaud yourself now, because at times during this first year you may feel like you are the only person that is applauding. Yet, you must continue to be positive and believe in yourself.

As a great first-year teacher, you will work very hard each day to help your students excel. You do this because you believe in your students and love your job. You will create new and innovative lessons to help motivate your students and create a positive learning atmosphere. Applaud yourself and be proud of your accomplishments.

You must realize that your students are a reflection of you. During your first year, the choir will begin to reflect your qualities and traits. By your third year, the choir *is* a reflection of you. So, when you are complimented, reply humbly with, "The choirs are great because I have the best students who work very hard," but know that after three years the choir is good because you are a good teacher. Then, applaud yourself for being awesome.

An Applause Savings Account

During your first year of teaching you will have major demands placed on your smaller-than-anticipated paycheck. Give to yourself by placing $75 to $100 per month in a special "applause saving account." During the spring, read your journals or look on the Internet to find a summer workshop, class or conference. This is a perfect tax-deductible vacation, and at the same time you are improving yourself professionally. In addition, it could give you additional hours to fulfill school district requirements in professional development or move you closer to your advanced degree. This "applause saving account" will let you have fun and reward you for your hard work.

You are going to be awesome teacher. Believe in yourself and give yourself the applause that you deserve.

A teacher affects eternity; he can never tell where his influence stops.

—Henry Brooks Adams

A good teacher is someone who directs and instructs, but never demands that a student learn. A good teacher challenges your mind and provides you with opportunities to gain knowledge at your own speed. A good teacher encourages you to ask questions, even if your ideas are not completely correct. A good teacher teaches from the heart with an inner sense of desire for others to enjoy the mysteries of the universe.

—Laura Medley

The Hat of a

Flamingo

15

The Hat of a

Flamingo

You have chosen one of the most fulfilling and rewarding careers available. To see the "light turn on" and the "I get it" look in the faces of your students who are seized with the excitement of learning is a feeling that can't be compared to anything else. You can make a difference in many students' lives. Now it is time for you to stick out your neck, flap your wings and fly, like a baby bird leaving its nest.

This chapter is devoted to the final pieces that will help ensure your success during your first year. These helpful tips include the personality traits of excellent teachers, the selection of music, handling stress, and the importance of laugher.

Personality Traits of Excellent Teachers

There are many characteristics that make one into a master teacher. The sixteen that appeared again and again as I observed master teachers are listed below. As a new teacher, occasionally review this list to check the traits that you possess and those you want to develop. Be aware that many personality traits develop with experience and maturity.

- Cooperativeness
- Creativity
- Dedication and willingness
- Democratic judgment
- Emotional stability
- Enthusiasm
- Hard work
- Individuality
- Intelligence
- Neat and distinctive appearance
- Organizational ability
- Positivism
- Receptivity to new ideas and situations
- Sense of humor
- Tolerance
- Warmth and friendliness

Music Selection

One of the major concerns of new teachers is how to find quality choral literature. In the book *Teaching Music in Today's Secondary Schools*, it is stated: "The success of many choral groups can be attributed partly to the careful selection of music literature. The search for suitable music is a difficult, time-consuming, never-ending process...It is imperative that the teacher examine and analyze all the music being considered in terms of its specific suitability."[1]

Unfortunately, some new teachers use their favorite eight-part university choral selections instead of selecting compositions for the ability level of their own choir. Literature needs to be chosen for the appropriate level of your choir, which may have eighteen members and only one tenor. Consideration must also be paid to age-appropriate texts and accessible accompaniments, to name but two.

Finding New Music to Evaluate
Sources of music to review include:

- Complimentary literature sent from music stores and publishing companies
- Choral workshops and clinics
- Publisher's exhibits and reading sessions at music conventions
- In-store stock of local and regional music stores
- Publisher CDs
- Publisher and music store approval packets
- Publisher new-music clubs
- Music teacher exchanges

---

[1] Malcolm Bessom, Alphonse Tatarunis and Samuel Forcucci, *Teaching Music in Today's Secondary Schools* (New York: Holt, Rinehart and Winston, 1980) 200.

- Attendance at music concerts given by performing organizations similar to your own
- Websites of music dealers and publishers

Stress

First-year teachers, when interviewed, were concerned about dealing with stress. When dealing with stress, it is important to remember that there are both good and bad stresses. Good stress can put you on that edge of excellence when performing, or give you that extra boost on the first day of school. Bad stress is the terrible pressure that one can put on one's self or can be inflicted by administration. At its worst, bad stress can create illness, mood changes and other problems that lead to the need for outside help or time off.

You must be extremely careful not to let bad stress control your life. Please remember that there is nothing wrong with asking for help from a medical professional, friend or colleague. Bad stress is correctable. Recognizing it and asking for help is often all it takes to begin addressing, and ultimately remedying, the problem.

I Think I'm Having Stress!—Twenty Ways to Cope

1. Get up 15 minutes earlier
2. Prepare for the morning the night before
3. Set appointments ahead of time
4. Make duplicate keys
5. Make copies of important papers
6. Repair anything that doesn't work properly
7. Ask for help on jobs you dislike

8. Have goals for yourself
9. Stop a bad habit
10. Ask someone to be your "vent partner"
11. Do it today
12. Plant a tree
13. Feed the birds
14. Stand and stretch
15. Memorize a joke
16. Exercise
17. Learn words to a new song
18. Get to work early
19. Clean out one closet
20. Write a note to a friend

Laughter

Laughing makes us feel better, breaks down barriers, and helps to solve problems. You must be willing to laugh—out loud and often—as a new teacher.

Every day you enter your classroom there is the potential for some great laughing moments. Focusing on the things you have seen, said, heard, and done could bring you to laughter. Think positively, smile and laugh. If you make a mistake, vow not to make the same one tomorrow, but keep on smiling and laughing.

Never let yourself get so low that you can't laugh. Remember, every teacher had a first year, and they all know that the second year is easier. On those tough days, or when you need a lift, consider these "Smiles."

Smile 1—Exam Papers of Students

- John Sebastian Bach died from 1750 to the present.
- A virtuoso is a musician with real high morals.
- Handel was half German, half Italian, and half English. He was rather large.
- Agnus Dei was a woman composer famous for her church music.
- Refrain means don't do it. A refrain in music is the part you better not try to sing.
- J.S. Bach was known for two important points: (A) His 21 children, and (B) His big organ.
- Beethoven wrote music even though he was deaf. He was so deaf he wrote loud music. He took long walks in the forest even when everyone was calling him. I guess he could not hear so good. Beethoven expired in 1827 and later dies from this.
- Henry Purcell is a well-known composer few people have ever heard of.
- J.S. Bach was a great musician because he practiced on his spinster in the attic.
- Aaron Copland is one of your most famous contemporary composers. It is unusual to be contemporary. Most composers do not live until they are dead.
- An opera is a song of bigly size.
- In the last scene of *Pagliacci*, Canio stabs Nedda who is the one he really loves. Pretty soon Silvio also gets stabbed, and they all live happily ever after.
- Probably the most marvelous fugue was the one between the Hatfields and the McCoys.
- My very best liked piece is the Bronze Lullaby.

- My favorite composer is Opus.
- A Harp is a nude piano.
- Most authorities agree that music of antiquity was written long ago.
- A good orchestra is always ready to play if the conductor steps on the odium.
- Music sung by two people at the same time is called a duel.
- I know what a sextet is, but my mother doesn't permit me to speak about that nasty subject.

Smile 2—Teachers Get Paid Too Much

I'm fed up with teachers and their hefty salary guides. What we need here is a little perspective. If I had my way, I'd pay these teachers myself...I'd pay them baby-sitting wages. That's right...instead of paying these outrageous taxes, I'd give them $3 an hour out of my own pocket. And I'm only going to pay them for five hours, not coffee breaks.

That would be $15 a day. Each parent should pay $15 a day for these teachers to baby-sit their child. Even if they have more than one child, it's still a lot cheaper than private day care.

Now, how many children do they teach a day—maybe twenty? That's $15 x 20 = $300 a day. But remember, they only work 180 days a year! I'm not going to pay them for all those vacation days. $300 x 180 = $54,000. (Just a minute, I think my calculator needs new batteries.)

I know…now you teachers will say, "What about those who have ten years' experience and a Masters degree?" Well, maybe (to be fair) they could get the minimum wage, and instead of just baby-sitting, they could read the kids a story. We can round that off to about $5 an hour x 5 hours x 20 children. That's $500 a day x 180 days. That's $90,000…HUH???????

Wait a minute. Let's get a little perspective here. Baby-sitting wages are too good for these teachers. Did anyone see a salary guide around here????

—Author Unknown

Smile 3—Excuses for Students from Parents

- Please excuse Chuck for being absent January 28, 29, 30, 31, 32, & 33.
- Chris has an acre in his side.
- June could not go to school because she was bothered by very close veins.
- Danny was absent yesterday because he had a stomach.
- Please excuse Stacy. She has been sick and under the Doctor.
- My son is under the Doctor's care and should not take P.E. Please execute him.
- Leslie was absent from school yesterday because she had a gang over.
- Please excuse Jason from P.E. for a few days. Yesterday he fell out of a tree and misplaced his hip.
- Please excuse Chris, Friday. He had loose vowels.

- Carlos was hit yesterday playing football. He was hit in the growing part.
- Please excuse Tiffany from Jim today. She is administrating.
- My daughter couldn't come to school Monday because she was tired. She spent the weekend with some Marines.
- Please excuse Megan from being absent yesterday. She was in bed with gramps.
- Miles was absent yesterday because of a sour trout.
- Please excuse David for being out yesterday. He had the fuel.
- Please excuse Jan for being absent. She was sick and I had her shot.
- Kip was absent this morning because he missed his bust.

Now stick out your neck, move to the edge of the nest, flap your wings, and fly! Be the best teacher in the world. You are the future of this fantastic profession. Now go out there and become a Master Music Teacher!

As teachers, we must believe in change, must know it is possible, or we wouldn't be teaching—because education is a constant process of change. Every single time you "teach" something to someone, it is ingested, something is done with it, and a new human being emerges.

—*Leo Buscaglia*

Appendix A

Resource Books for Producing a Musical

American Song—The Complete Musical Theatre Companion
Kenneth Bloom
Facts on File Publications, 1996

Broadway Musicals: Show by Show, 5th edition
Stanley Green
Hal Leonard Books, 1997

Encyclopedia of Music Theatre
Stanley Green
Da Capo Press, 1991

Encyclopedia of Musical Theatre
Kurt Ganzi
Blackwell Publishers, 1994

*Musicals! A Directory of Musical Properties Available for
    Production*
Richard Chigley Lynch
American Library Association, 1985

Stage it with Music: An Encyclopedic Guide to the American Theatre
Thomas S. Hinchak
Greenwood Publishing Group Inc., 1995

Stage Lighting Step-By-Step—The Complete Guide on Setting the Stage with Light to Get Dramatic Results
Graham Walters
Betterway Books, 1997

Stage Scenery—Its Construction and Rigging
A.S. Gillette and J. Michael Gillette
Harper and Row Publishers, 1981

Staging Music Theatre—A Complete Guide for Directors
Elaine A. Novak and Deborah Novak
Betterway Books, 1996

About the Author

Dr. Richard Weymuth is a native of Cole Camp, Missouri. He began his career in 1967 and taught vocal music from the kindergarten to university level until his retirement in 2001.

Dr. Weymuth moved to his last position at Northwest Missouri State University in 1980. As Director of Choirs and professor of music, he not only directed the Northwest Celebration, Tower Choir and Madraliers, but also taught courses in secondary choral methods, choral conducting and applied voice. His administrative duties included: Director of the Northwest Summer Music Camps, Director of the 48-school Northwest

Jazz and Show Choir Festival, Choral Director of University Musicals, and Producer of the Northwest Yuletide Feastes.

He received his B.M.E. and M.A. degrees from Central Missouri State University in Warrensburg, and his Ph.D. from the University of Miami in Coral Gables, Florida. His dissertation title was *The Development and Evaluation of a Cognitive Music Achievement Test to Evaluate Missouri High School Choral Music Students.*

Dr. Weymuth is a past president of Missouri American Choral Directors Association, a past vice president of the Missouri Music Educators Association, and a past president of Missouri Student Music Educators Association. In 2002, he was the thirtieth inductee to the Missouri Music Hall of Fame. He is only the fourth choral director to be inducted. In 1992, he received the Luther T. Spayde Award from the Missouri American Choral Directors Association as the Outstanding Choral Director of the Year. He was named Outstanding Music Alumni of the Year in 1981 by Central Missouri State University and has received honors from the National Junior Chamber of Commerce as an Outstanding Young Man in America.

In the fall of 1992, Dr. Weymuth was one of six choral conductors from the United States selected to participate in the International Choral Directors Music Exchange with Sweden. He spent two weeks touring Sweden and working with their outstanding choral ensembles.

Dr. Weymuth is the author of *Selected Renaissance Literature for the High School Choir*, a resource published by Laudamus Press. He is also a contributing author to *Getting Started with Jazz/Show Choir*, edited by Russell L. Robinson and published by Music Educators National Conference. His choral editions are available from various publishers.

Along with his teaching and directing achievements, Dr. Weymuth is known for his numerous junior and senior high school choral clinics. During the past years, he has conducted over 700 choral clinics and festivals. He has conducted major choral festivals and all-state choirs in 39 states. Dr. Weymuth is also known for his numerous national and regional workshops on classroom motivation, student leadership, success in the classroom, choral literature, and show choir techniques.

Dr. Weymuth's wife, Annelle, was the Executive Assistant to the President at Northwest Missouri State University. She completed her Ph.D. at the University of Missouri-Columbia in Human Development and Family Studies. She is a past state president of the Missouri Home Economics Association, and currently the state president of American Association of University Women. Annelle and Rick have a son and daughter-in-law, who live in Columbus, Indiana. They are the proud parents of Rick and Annelle's first grandchild, Olivia Nicole Weymuth, born May 24, 2002.